THE GINGERBREAD MAN

An Autobiography

FRED WELCH

Drawings
By the author

iUniverse, Inc.
New York   Bloomington

The Gingerbread Man
An Autobiography

iUniverse books may be ordered through booksellers or by contacting:

iUniverse
1663 Liberty Drive
Bloomington, IN 47403
www.iuniverse.com
1-800-Authors (1-800-288-4677)

Because of the dynamic nature of the Internet, any Web addresses or links contained in this book may have changed since publication and may no longer be valid. The views expressed in this work are solely those of the author and do not necessarily reflect the views of the publisher, and the publisher hereby disclaims any responsibility for them.

ISBN: 978-1-4401-1160-0 (sc)
ISBN: 978-1-4401-1164-8 (hc)
ISBN: 978-1-4401-1161-7 (ebook)

Printed in the United States of America

iUniverse rev. date: 1/12/09

About the Author

Fred Welch, was born in Bay St. Louis, Ms. August 14th, 1936. Although you could say he traveled and lived in almost all the coastal towns along. He is the second child of Timothy H. and Edith Ansley Welch – along with his two sisters, who have at this writing, have gone on to their heavenly rewards, and one brother who lives and makes his home on the west coast of California.

Fred's education came about at the hands and rulers of the Sisters of Mercy at St. John's in Gulfport, MS, Jr. College at Gulf Coast Junior College, and a two plus two in union with University of Southern MS – a course in the principles and practices of Urban Planning. He is a single parent from the mid 70's to completion, raising two sons and two daughters, the gift of all the Grandchildren not raised by me – nine grandchildren and two Great Grandchildren.

Fred is the author of his first book, *A Call to Holiness*, published in 2007. It is a personal, mystical writing of his spiritual journey – a book he hopes pleases his God and those who read it too!

Fred is an accomplished musician, playing the classical guitar and much prefers jazz and the standards. He has worked in clay and sculpture and fine art. He teaches music and theory and art in private lessons. He loves his church, St. Thomas the Apostle in Long Beach, Mississippi, his pastor Fr. Louis Lohan and most of the people who attend there too!

Note from Fred:

I find at a young age of 72 to be in complete wonder every day of my life at life itself. I love God's animals and sunsets and sunrises. I miss my black Lab Vincent, who is chasing cats somewhere in Heaven!

I hope you enjoy my book

Fred Welch
Author

ACKNOWLEDGMENTS:

To God for all the many gifts He as loaned me,
My two sons, Joe and Chris, for their love and support,
Silvia and Brooke, for word processing and correcting all
my bad spelling,
My brother Michael Welch and to
In Memory of Father J. Joseph Buttimer(1933-2002)

DEDICATION:

To God, for all the gifts He has loaned me.
To my maternal grandmother, Florence C. Ansley, my first
teacher,
To my mother and father, who most all my life I tried
desperately to find favor with.

All you that are righteous,
Shout for joy for what the Lord has done;
Praise Him, all you that obey Him,
Give thanks to the Lord with harps,
Sing to Him with stringed instruments.
Sing new songs to Him.
Play the harp with skill,
And shout for Joy!

Psalm 33

About the Book *The Gingerbread Boy* by Richard Scarry

This wonderful book has done wonders for many young children - it taught them to be afraid and cautious of wolves - the four legged and the two legged kind - the dark, and water, and trust and so on!

However, children have to be scared of things, especially if they are in some environment like their bedroom, or a tree house, or where Mom and Dad can hear their screams and such - go figure. I believe Mr. Scarry had figured this out before he put pen to paper.

CHAPTERS

PREFACE

Listen, when I began this manuscript 38 years ago, it was to be a birthday present for my 55th year. Now at the age of 72, I finally decided to submit this book for publication. About 28 or so years ago, as I was having dinner with some friends, one of them began to ask me about myself and where did I grow up. I was sort of taken aback. These were, for the most part, people I had known for forty or so years.

It then occurred to me that some of them really did not know too much about me and the life I was before I met most of them. As I explained, my coming into being with as much humor as I could get by with, I began to think that maybe I should keep some kind of journal, or at least write it all down. When I got home later that evening, I, not being of the computer and internet world, had to recourse to pen and paper. I would write as I dug into my memory banks. I was surprised to remember things that for many years, I had not even thought about.

Now as a man in his early seventies and of questionable health, I wondered for what good it would do me as almost all of my immediate family had long ago gone to their heavenly rewards. At this June 2007 writing there is only my brother, Michael, five years my junior. Well, the more I seemed to recall, the more I entertained the thought of writing a *tell all* book, so to speak. My brother Michael is still too angry and burdened down with a lot of family baggage to really deal with his demons. I, on the other hand seem to find it all very amusing and sad.

I actually look upon the writing of this story as very liberating and cleansing. We are for the most part a product of nature and nurturing. I certainly do not pretend to be an expert in this department, but who, I ask you, has a better perspective than me? I was there and this is a peephole version of what I saw, or thought I saw.

A Wolf, and I cannot speak for yours, is that thing that haunts us and gets in the way of our ability to get the most out of this journey called life. It will, if it can stifle and repress us and keep us from being the who we were meant to be. Let me say here and now that no matter whom I write about - or who, I do not dislike or hold resentments or any anger or malice to them. I would like to think that I have now overcome all that petty and negative stuff that keeps us tied up in knots. We spend most of our life getting our rope tied up in knots, then pay good money to someone to help us get them all out.

The use of products and famous people and things is in no way meant to disparage the fine product and symbols of these fine items. Nor references made to certain people - I miss and care deeply for most of them. The title, *The Gingerbread Man* is one I came up with over 30 years ago. It seemed to me at the time an appropriate way to explain the different telling of my journeys and situations - the sugars, the spices, and the salts of life and how it affected me.

This is the story about me. Some of you may have heard this and some may have heard that, but no one has ever heard the real story from me or come to think about it, no one has ever asked me about me. We wait, like most people until it's too late. Fear, I guess or something like it, keeps us from knowing the real person. Well, since no one has asked me, I will tell you anyway. Before I get too far ahead I want to say that I think of my life as being lived in at least three different lives in three time zones.

I will use whatever visual aids as I may have - pictures, notes, cards, etc.

So, please turn the page and let the gingerbread man take you on a spicy journey.

However, do watch out for the Wolf!

INTRODUCTION

I believe that in writing this book I will somehow clear out, or throw out all the mental junk I have collected traveling down the Road of life. I am only keeping what I will call the good and useful stuff. God knows what that will be! I do not intend to look back over my shoulder as I do this, for I am certain my path will be littered with much castaway debris, and I do not need a second look at any of it anymore.

As to my mother and father this book's intention is not to discredit them in any way, more so it's to show them as and what they were, simply seekers, searchers of themselves and life - not perfect but like all of us - with feet of clay - giving, selfish, weak, strong at times, fearful, simply human. Anyway this book is not about them, but me! It's my peephole version of what I see or think I see! It's my gift to me, my 55th birthday present to me - an age at times I believed I would never see.

The crude drawings in this book are mine. It will give you some idea of how far I've progressed in my growth - spiritually, physically, and sexually. Do not hold any high hopes! I certainly do not, at least until I clean out the attic, so to speak.

A special thanks to Kurt Vonnegut, Jr., who by the way knows nothing of or about the writing of this book. His contribution is for messing up my head by reading anything and everything I could get my hands on that he had written over the past 25 or so years - for stirring in me the belief that I may have something to say! And a way to say it! Talk about how easy some of us can be lead astray.

Also, this book's title is not to be misinterpreted with the fine children's book by a like name, *The Gingerbread Boy:* by Richard Scarry. Actually the only common thread may be the wolf that wants to eat the gingerbread boy.

My Wolf had other ideas!

Author
   Fred Welch

The
Gingerbread
Man

From Webster's Dictionary

Special notes on use:

Gingerbread (Webster's) - A dark molasses cake flavored with ginger, a soft molasses and ginger cookie, cut in various shapes, sometimes with frosting.

Gypsy (Roma) - one of a nomadic Caucasoid people originally migrating from the border region between Iran and India to Europe in the 14th and 15th century, and now living in mostly Europe and the United States.

Paper: Pulp - A mixture of cellulose material, such as wood, rags, and other paper ground up to make a pulp. A thin sheet material made of the pressed and dried pulp used chiefly for writing, packaging, and such.

Beaver - A large aquatic rodent of the genus Castor, having thick brown fur, webbed feet, a paddle-like hairless tail, and chisel-like teeth adapted for gnawing bark and felling trees to build dams.

Virgin - A person who has not expressed or experienced sexual intercourse.

3

Fred Welch

American Indian - A member or native of the original inhabitants of North America.

Whiskey - Alcoholic liquor distilled from grain, such as corn, rye, or barley and containing approximately 40 to 50 % ethyl alcohol.

General Electric - A company whose sole purpose is to market things that people think they cannot live without.

U.S. Bach - 1685-1750 German composer and organist - father of four sons who were also composers.

Staph Infection - Any of the various Gram-positive spherical parasitic bacteria of the genus Staphylococcus, occurs in grape-like clusters causing boils, Septicemia, and other infections.

Yeast - Any of the various unicellular fungi of the genus Saccharomyces and related genera, reproducing by budding and capable of fermenting carbohydrates.

Description of paper and ink, what makes them:

Ink: is ground earth pigment with a medium and binder to make it flow.

Paper: is ground up wood products with chemicals that make it easier to form into large sheets of this and that kind of writing paper, and so on.

Genesis

"Hop on my back," said the wolf to the boy, and "I'll give you a ride across the lake!"

How else was the boy to get across I ask you?

Well, I sat by the edge of the lake and dreamed of the other side. How I longed to see the other side. But I could not discount the wolf, there in the lake, watching, just waiting for me to make up my mind for a ride, or a mistake.

So, I sat there with one eye on the other side of the lake and with the other on the Wolf!

THE BEGINNING
MY FIRST LIFE

August 14, 1936 – Had you asked my mother, she would
have told you I was a most difficult birth. She once told me
that she was in labor for about three days, and then I had
to be taken out of her womb. If I had the ability of reason
or thought, I could have been more prepared for my life to
come. A lot has been written about *Nature vs. Nurture*, and
how it plays in our outcome and development.

I was born to Edith May Ansley and Timothy H. Welch,
my mother being almost three years older than my father.
She is from a coastal community family from Bay St. Louis,
Mississippi. Her mother, my Grandmother, is a Capdepon
of French, Italian, and Russian heritage. My mother's father,
Fred Ansley, is of English and Irish blood.

My father was born into a country family and raised on a
farm until the age of 16 or so. When he left to make his way
in the world there were 13 brothers and sisters in his family
but like most rural families of his time they were close. He
said his father was strict but I did not see my Grandfather
Joseph Henry Welch in that way. I had great affection for my
grandfather.

Delphie M. Carter, my paternal grandmother was a good, hardworking woman, mostly set to the quiet. She loved to cook and care for her large family. My great grandfather on my father's side is of Scotch-Irish and Indian blood. From time to time I will refer back to them. In my immediate family were my mother and father, my brother Michael H. Welch, two sisters: Mary Anne Welch (Bell), and Shannon Marie (Hernandez), (Meter), (Markell), (Pigg) and these are just some of them I either met or briefly knew of. My mother and father have gone on to their rest in 1982-83, then my older sister in July of 1985. Shannon Marie went on to her rest November 11, 2005, two months after Hurricane Katrina leveled the Gulf Coast of Mississippi.

My maternal Grandmother, Florence Capdepon-Ansley lived in our home until she died in July of 1946. She was a victim of breast cancer in a time when treatments were difficult and hard to find. I remember the many car trips to Mobile, Alabama to get radiation treatments, the treatment of the day at that time. She lost the fight in spite of it all. She died in her room in our house one summer day. I remember it well. She was really the glue that made us a family. I love and miss her to this very day. She was the Norman Rockwell type of Grandmother you hear and visualize. There were trips to the park, movies and walks and talks for my older sister and me. I'm sure she loved Mike and Shannon too, but this story is about me and the events that came to be, the me I am or not!

My early memories are of a time I think to be in Bay St. Louis, MS. I may be three or four years of age. Someone is wearing a Halloween mask and it frightens me and I begin to cry. I think maybe my mother is holding me. I see wood floors and old wood doors. Then my next memory is being in Gulfport on 25th Ave or St., where the old Eastward School used to be. Across is now a McDonald's fast food. We lived in an old house that was next all to close to the home of the

Barnetts' who had a floor finishing business. I do know that our family and theirs did not get along at all. The homes are still there but have been joined together to make one. Even the old tree in front is still there. I used to climb in and pretend I was Tarzan of the Apes. I also shot a slingshot with a marble at the son of one of the Barnett's, smack between the eyes! His older sister chased me back under an old home. She promised me a lot of things to get me out – finally I did. She gave me a spanking. Today that would be child abuse and she would go to jail or prison. I remember some older kids took the wheels off of my peddle-car and both mom and dad gave me heck for that.

We even took in borders to make ends meet. I remember one lady who had the flu or a real bad cold. She let me look at the stuff she coughed up, not a very pretty sight. It was also during this time that Mary Anne and myself shared all the childhood ailments of the time: measles, mumps, chicken pox, and whooping cough.

Sometime later, my family probably wary and tired of dealing with the Barnetts' bought a home on 19th Ave with my Grandmother's help and money. It was bought mostly with the money and US savings bonds saved by my Grandmother. She worked for Bell Telephone for over 30 years. She started as an operator in Bay St. Louis and then worked in Gulfport until retirement. I remember well the retirement dinner and party. It was given at the old Great Southern Hotel in downtown Gulfport. I think at this writing it is now the home of several small businesses, lawyers, real estate and a coffee house and whatever. In its hay day the Great Southern was mostly constructed of wood and took up the complete block – 13th St to the beach, Hwy 90. It was also during this time my Grandmother developed breast cancer. A fight she would lose in 1946.

They did a lot of work remodeling it and I liked it a lot. I remember while they were working on it, I fell backwards in the exposed floor juices and hit the back of my head, which made a real big bump. I also had my feet find any exposed rusty nails they could find.

I grew up in a time of no TV. I had only radio and the ability to amuse myself with my imagination. We had an old Philco radio – one the size of a small washing machine. In the evenings after supper we sat around and watched radio using our minds to make the pictures of the peoples' events.

I'm now around eight or nine and the Second World War is going on. WWII they called it. Everything was rationed according to size and family. You received rations of stamps, gas and tires for a car, if you had one. There were also rations for butter, milk and things. Even at the age of eight or nine years, hearing of the things happening to the Jews made me very sad! I wondered why the people of the world, and especially America, did not put a stop to the slaughter of the Jewish people.

Our home was always busy with uncles, aunts, cousins, Great Grandmother (Josephine Capdepon), Great Aunts Vera and Gertie. By the way, Aunt Vera raised Uncle Gussie's kids, Carol and Violet. Uncle Gussie Capdepon did not want to raise them. His wife was named Rita, Rite for short. I'm not sure she died a young woman. There is a marble history of these people in St. Mary's Cemetery in Bay St. Louis, next to St. Rose de Lima Catholic Church.

I did not get to know my Grandfather on my mother's side. He and my Grandmother had separated. His name was Fred Ansley, from the Ansley community west of Bay St. Louis and was a bugler in the First World War. I only remember seeing him two times. I was only ten or eleven the last time. He lived and died in Los Angeles, Ca. He is buried in the Westwood Veterans cemetery.

I really believe the home on 19th Ave. was haunted. There were strange things that went on there like bumps and banging. I had real bad nightmares at night and saw very spooky things. One time I woke to see the most grizzly, ugly, old woman with – I thought – hair on fire, railing to beat at me with her arms stretched up and screaming at me. I shared this with my sister Mary Anne. She said she also saw this same vision from time to time. When I had these nightmares I would get up and go to my Grandmother's room. She had put a cot at the end of her bed. She would ask me what was wrong and I told her. She would let me sleep on the cot at her feet. I never felt so safe, loved and wanted, even to this day. Did I mention that I thought her to be the oldest person on the earth? When she finally lost the battle with cancer she was only 52 years of age. When my sister died she was only 52. Also, I miss them both quite a bit.

Now in the home of 19th Ave I had my first spiritual experiences. (See my first book, *A Call to Holiness*.) Homes at that time all had open front porches with chairs, rockers and a swing. In the back of our home was a full half wood-half screen porch. I spent most of my time there playing. You see I did not know anyone who had central a/c of any kind. They had attic fans and maybe a window fan. All homes had high ceilings. This home is still there in 19th Ave and in good shape.

My father being the good countryman he was always had dogs, ducks, chickens and grew vegetables. One time, if you can believe it, I went with him way out on 28th St. to buy a milk cow. I remember walking home with him. He would milk the cow every morning before he went to work at the Gulfport Laundry. He had a dry cleaning route and this set in motion a later event of him starting his own businesses all along the coast. My dad also grew flowers to sell. When it came to all saints day, mostly mums, people came from all over to buy them. He was also a very good mandolin player and played some guitar. When he was growing up in Laurel and Ellisville on the weekends he and his brothers, sisters, my uncles and cousins got together to play. They also played all Sunday at Mount Olive Baptist Church. It was an all day event. I went there with them and Mary Anne because we spent most summers out in the country. Mom and Dad sent us up there to lessen the possibility of getting polio. Back then there was no vaccine or treatment. Many people got it when summer came about. I will write more about this later.

My Observations about My Mother!

As you can see, I dress hurt and pain and disappointment in a suit of humor. I had to learn this real fast living with my two alcoholic parents. Did I mention they liked to drink, too? Not Stillbrook Whiskey, but wine and beer. My father liked to drink Rot Gutt, the kind made in stills – way out of the woods. It gave him such a glow. It also changed his disposition – mine too. I did without supper many times. Much too dangerous to venture out.

"Mr. Wolf, What strange behavior you do have!"

We had large clay urns on our two concrete porch steps – one on each side. Once my mother, under the influence of a fine wine made by the Gallo Brothers, came to believe she possessed the strength of Samson. You see the wine had deceived her brain into believing this untruth. She came out and like the Biblical man of strength, pushed both urns off the ledges of the side rails, smashing them in pieces.

Although I do not drink, then or even now, I was mildly impressed with this feat my mother had demonstrated for all of us – and some nosey neighbors – to see and laugh at!

Lucky ole us, you bet!! The Wolf sleeps!

Fred Welch

Sr. Wallberger or Why To This Day I Cannot Pee in Public!

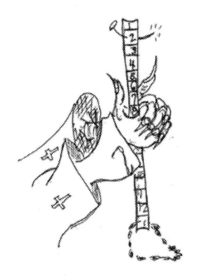

She loved to use this on some unsuspecting child, mostly us boys. I do not miss you Sr. Wallberger, is it very hot where you are?

As I may have said before, my sister Mary Ann, my older sister, whose peephole closed in 1985, and I began our education at St. John's m Gulfport, Mississippi around 1939-1940. At first I was mostly happy and eager to learn things that would serve me well later in life! I would like to say here that the nuns of Sisters of *Mercy* were in large part a great mystery to my friends and me. The habits, as they were called, that all nuns at that time wore was to us a symbol and fearful looking-all in long black garments and veils of the same black covering all of them except for the band of white around the face and neck. Black shoes, I guess, for we used to wonder and think that they didn't really walk like us, but float across the room or where they wanted to go, always with that ruler in their hands, looking for some unsuspecting youth to swat their open hands or knuckles. Most of all them had those long rosary beads that hung at their waist, clattering and rattling at every move - seemed to be an alarm system to alert us of impending doom.

This really did happen to me!

Back in school at St. John's in about 1942, I was in the 2nd grade. At that time at St. John's there were two grades in one room. First and Second were together and one nun taught both classes. Well, it was getting very close to time to leave for the day, but my kidneys had other ideas. We were taught to hold our hands up to be recognized and then the sister would ask what you wanted. I really had to go. So I asked if I could be excused. Sister glared at me and told me to sit down. I tried to forget the pressing need of my bladder. So I waited a few minutes more and held my hand up again. Sister looked at me and I asked to be excused. I was told to sit down. I now began to squirm and twist in my seat. I really had to go. Then I could hold it no longer and out it came all over my seat, the floor, and me. I was so embarrassed and ashamed. Next to me was a girl I thought was so very cute. The other kids just laughed and snickered and whispered to each other. When the bell rang I just sat there and waited for the other kids to leave. I didn't want to look at any of them.

I am now a man of 71 years and I am still embarrassed about that accident. I suppose I always will be. That's why

I do not like to pee in a public place. *God bless you Sister Wallberger.*

"GREAT-GRANDMOTHER, WHAT BIG EYES YOU HAVE!"

My great-grandmother came from Austria as a young married woman of 14 years old. My great-grandfather was from France. Like most all European immigrants of their day, they came to America with high hopes and dreams! Too bad their dreams betrayed them into thinking Bay St. Louis, Mississippi would be fertile ground to sow dream seeds in the late 1890's. They did, however, achieve a measure of success to some degree. My great-grandmother opened a neighborhood grocery store, owned property, and raised a large family of eleven children, five girls and six boys. Great-grandfather was with the railroad.

I remember Sunday trips from the Coast to Bay St. Louis. To me, as a kid, it seemed to take all day to drive there - at 35 mph The smells of the house; the chicken file' gumbo that was always cooked, and strong black coffee - coffee and chicory blend so black and dark I believe it could be put into fountain

pens and used instead of ink! To say there were strange people on my mother's side of the family would be some kind of understatement. My great Uncle Son - Son Capdepon - was a good example. The back yard had little grass to speak of, mostly bare dirt. Son would rake the ground smooth putting rake and tine marks in a pattern over all the bare earth. Then dare anyone to walk or put a footprint on the ground. My mother did as a young girl and he came after her with an axe! Talk about Lizzie Borden!

He once told me that if I kept looking at him he would cut off one of my ears and wear it on his watch chain. I believed him, too! He told me the same thing every time he saw me, all the time reaching into his pocket and bringing out his pocketknife.

When Uncle Son's peephole closed, they found in a wooden trunk in his bedroom, over $65,000 dollars in cash. He didn't trust banks. He also never owned a car, radio, TV, or electricity! Imagine that! He was married to a woman named Tootsie. She died six months after him. Distant relatives came of the money, property and all that they had. They had cars, radio, TV, and electricity, and a lot more.

My Uncle Son's trunk with a lot of loot inside!

Most all the sons of great-grandmother did well, and some of the girls, too! My great-grandmother lived to be 84 years old. Her peephole closed in 1956, the year I was married to 'Liz. When she died, she had poor eyesight and only one tooth in her head. It was on the bottom. She looked like this:

Cousin Pete and me killed all of Great-grandmother's chickens she raised in her backyard. We tied their feet together so they couldn't run and fed them to the two pigs she kept in pens out back!

I never told her I did this terrible thing! I never told anyone until now! I'm still ashamed of this crazy act.

 This is what her chickens looked like before Pete and I changed them.

I think I must not have liked my great-grandmother too much or myself!

Why are you so angry, Gingerbread Man? WHY?

ROLE MODELS

I didn't believe myself to be much different than other boys or girls. Growing up today, just as yesterday, they have a certain type of person or persons that impact and impress them during their growing periods. I was no different.

I suppose our parents are our first role models. After all, they are the ones first responsible for our primal needs: food, shelter, warmth, clothes, love, guilt and safety, the last one being of most importance.

My first role models were the cowboys on the big screen, Roy Rogers and Trigger. They were my heroes! And a woman named Florence Capderon Ansley, my maternal Grandmother.

Families back when I was a boy had one mother, one father, several brothers and sisters, usually a grandmother and or grandfather, an occasional aunt, or uncle and cousins living or dropping in for some time to time – at any time, all the time!

My family had a Mom, a Dad, Grandmother, two sisters, and one brother. We were happy as clams. Peas in a pod, so the speak. At least to me, at that time it seemed so. Conflict sets in later in life when adolescence rears its ugly head. We're never really content or at peace from that time on. There seems to be something missing until another wondrous thing occurs. These phenomena, this awakening, that light bulb suddenly lights up in our heads, hearts and soul and makes most things a bit more clear – but not all. Boy, talk about your insight!

Well, back to Florence, my Grandmother who taught me most of the life values and attitudes I now possess. At that time she seemed to me old and wise as Methuselah – maybe older – She cared for, loved, talked, and shared most of my childhood memories I now hold dear. I will write about Mary Ann, my sister, the first born of our family in another chapter. A book wouldn't be enough time to talk about her, but I'll share more later. She got a bad deal genetically speaking, just like Lucy, my ex-wife. Lucy was the mother of my children who looked like Liz Taylor, by mostly her family, who had bad wiring and bad chemicals in her brain.

Ginger Plant

My Grandmother would take us to the movies, to the park, shopping, or just to walk and talk. She had a secret plot going on in her body that she did not know was there at the time. She would find out later that her cells had decided to replicate for no apparent reason. Make war, and attack her vital organs. Their first objective would be one of her breasts. Then, later, there would be an all out assault on her body. She was defenseless. This ancient, wise, wonderful woman would surrender, so to speak, to this enemy on November 24, 1946 at 3 p.m., at the ripe old age of 52. Imagine that! I was 9 1/2.

Talk about Ginger!

So there! Listen, I said the only skills and values I learned were from my grandmother. Her peephole closed when she was 52 and I was only 9. We covered a lot, but never got around to sex. Sex to me just wasn't important at that time. Who knew I was going to marry Liz, I sure didn't. Not even her family knew. It's good they didn't for I believe they would have moved to another state had they known! Time is merciful and kind - to both of us. Ignorance is bliss, once said a wise man. I think him to be right. So, Lucy and I trudged on, me, the proud bread winner, Lucy the mother of children and maker of bad wiring and chemicals. Who knew? I sure didn't have a clue. Well, maybe I was deceiving myself! Imagine that!

Lucy made a lot of spur of the moment trips back to the Mississippi coast during this time. My, oh my! Hello. Goodbye! Again! "Pack my bags, cares, and woe. Here I go, singing low. Bye, Bye, Blackbird."

"Something Fishey"

About My Older Sister

Mary Ann was the firstborn, August 3, 1934 in Bay St. Louis, Mississippi. Not much left of that town since Katrina came through. She was born in a home my parents were living in at the time, now a school for ballet and tap dancing. My sister, by the way, was a very good dancer. We danced together and won many dance contests. The Boogie, Jitter Bug, and the Fox Trot were some of the popular dances of the time.

As children growing up she was my hero! I would believe anything she told me, even if I knew better. We had all the childhood diseases of the time. Measles, mumps, chicken pox, and whooping cough - you name it. Yep, we had it together.

I could write a book on all the stuff she talked me into doing, most of what got me in hot water with my mother and father. She could lie with more conviction than anyone I know, more than a politician or lawyer.

One time she came up to me by the living room window. Now at those times homes did not have *a/c* systems, window fans yes. All homes, or most, had high ceilings at least 10 feet high and plenty of windows. My Grandmother liked to have a lot of sheer, lacy curtains with large vases by each side on the floor. In those vases were fluffy cattails. They were long, very dry, and highly volatile. Well, in comes Mary Ann with box of safety head matches. She looked at the fluffy cattails and me, pursed her lips and said this to me: "Brother, I bet you cannot strike this match and place it by the cattails before they catch fire." Well, I knew better, but she had as I said before, this spell she could cast on me. So, off I go on this challenge to my boyhood. Yep! Up went the cattails, curtains, and some of the woodwork too! I stood there in total disbelief. My mind was a complete blur.

I thought of leaving home or joining the circus. If I would have known what an out of body experience was, I would have prayed for that too! There went Mary Ann with a smug look on her face as she walked away. She said over her shoulder: "Boy, I would hate to be in your shoes when mom and dad get home." I'll spare you most of the details, but if you ever saw the movie airplane with the scene about the hysterical person that everyone was lining up to slap, beat, and pound this unfortunate individual - well, that was I so to speak! But you know I gladly take a whipping like that, to spend just one day with my older sister whose peephole closed on July 8, 1985. I wonder if she is getting anyone in trouble in heaven? She loved music and rocking chairs. I have hers with me now.

As I stop and turn around and look back at my path and the salts and spices of my journey, I see this and that that I have cast over my shoulder, odd though, I have not rid myself of all the mental clunk and stuff I have accumulated over this lifetime. Maybe it takes even more time, effort and honesty than I created for myself. There are other people, places and events I have not written about. Like Ray Winterstien, my childhood and teen years' friend. There were whiskey sours and bus trips to the hot spot for strippers and jazz music and trying to get home before the last bus run on the beach from Gus Steven's. We were 13 years old, on his untimely death, two weeks before he was to be married at the age of 19!

Many childhood and schoolmates have gone on to their final reward. A lot of peepholes closed.

Moving,
Or
It's Just the Gypsy in My Soul

As best as I can figure it out, my Mother and Father were:
1) Restless, 2) Very unhappy everywhere they went, 3) or
owed the IRS and the CIA something BIG. By the time I
was seven they had moved 8 or 9 times. Honest Indian! And
more moves to come, too. No grass will ever lie under their
feet. No Sir! But they only migrated along the coastline of
Mississippi and the Louisiana border, sort of like sea birds.
They could have had good jobs with the Wildlife and Fisheries
Department, but they were not into saving the planet or
wildlife or anything except their asses. All they wanted to do
was get away from themselves and each other, real fast. Save
their own asses, so to speak. Fat chance! "Those far away
places I've been reading (dreaming) about in a book that I
took from the shelf."

My Father finally quieted his wanderlust for the time to go
to work for a laundry and dry cleaning establishment named
"Gulfport Laundry and Cleaning Co." owned by Mr. Bill
Alberts. He came by the business through his Father, William
Alberts, Sr., who really founded the company and did all the

dirty work, so to speak. Talk about luck, talk about being in the right place at the right time. After my Father learned this bit of Alberts' family history and success story, his lust for power, money, and success blotted out all rational thinking. Nothing would do. He must have his own business and that was that! Of course he invested fourteen years with Gulfport Laundry, before his thirst for power and his own business finally drove him to go for it! *My Dad, the dreamer.*

Mother had dreams about other things, but they were not cleaning other people's dirty clothes! Not by a long shot! Edith Ansley Welch was disappointed with marital bliss. She wanted something more out of life, namely a husband that talked *to* her *not at* her. Just call me co-dependent.

How many people do you know that own a home, free and clear at the age of 26? My Dad did. Of course he had considerable help from my maternal grandmother. She was a saver! She worked all her life for the phone company. She started working for Southern Bell Telephone Co. in Bay St. Louis when my mother was just a small girl- after my maternal grandfather, Fred Ansley, the artist, the musician, the womanizer, the child molester, the sex crazed man about town, threw them out, left them flat! How about them apples! My grandmother could squeeze a nickel until the buffalo doo-doo'd on the Indian on the other side. We used to have nickels like that. Fred Ansley is defunct, his peephole closed in 1956, and somewhere around the time I married Liz. Life sure is mysterious. He's resting now in Los Angeles Veteran's Cemetery in Westwood. I've been there. It's a military cemetery! He was a sergeant in the Drum and Bugle Corps. *Root-a-toot-toot* played the bugle!

Look back to my frugal Grandmother. She pinched, saved, bought stock, bought savings bonds, war bonds, and God knows what all. She invested, and had bank accounts. When my Dad found out about all this stored up wealth, he fixed all his energies on fleecing her out of it for his pipe dreams - his desire to clean things up, so to speak.

Besides his 26 chromosomes, I also inherited some of his lusts, pipe dreams, and itchy feet. "Follow the yellow brick road!" and so on! "We're off to see the wizard, the wonderful Wizard of Oz."

PiPE DREAMS!

No One Knows
the Trouble I've Seen

My parents' itchy feet took them to Long Beach after the failure of my father's Dry Cleaning and Laundry business. Oh well, easy come, easy go. I wonder what Grandmother would think of all that, and where her life savings went.

We lived in an old home on 1st Street, south of the railroad tracks. Back then we were considered poor and not well-to-do. Now being south of the railroad tracks would be different.

The home was modest and most of our family, Mom, Dad, two sisters, a younger brother, and myself, fit here and there, so to speak. Wood frame and wood siding, the paint on the outside was several coats thick and probably held enough lead to alter the mental growth of a small village. One thing I did enjoy about living there was the sound and smell of the old steam locomotives belching out huge clouds of gray-black smoke and the chug-chug of the pistons driving the wheels on the tracks. You could hear them coming way off in the distance. I would run to see them every time I heard them. The locomotive horn had a distinct sound, breathy and belching smoke! This will be one of the memories I will tuck away and keep.

Another will be the long deserted wood structure that was known as the old packing shed. It was next to our property line. This shed was 500 feet long and maybe 50 feet wide. Long since left to natured ruin, it was built to house vegetables and the like, back when Long Beach was known as Rosalie Station.

When it was daylight, we, I and other boys of my age, would explore the ruins and things left long forgotten. That was at daylight. At night, it took on a more foreboding and eerie look. As there were no street lights between our home and the main street of Jeff Davis Ave. to the West. I remember well when I did go to Gulfport, a town to the East of Long Beach, to see a movie. This was a time when there were no TV's and any entertainment was an occasional house party or a movie in Gulfport. You had to catch a city bus and hope you did not miss the one coming back after the movie let out. The buses stopped running at midnight on the dot. At this time there were scary movies, *The Mummy, The Wolf Man,* and of course the *Frankenstein* movies with Boris Karloff.

Coming back, after I departed the bus, I had that long, dark, and very scary stretch to get home. How I hated that shed! I would walk slowly at first, then about halfway, at the darkest place, I would feel my heart pound and I could imagine all sorts of beasts in and around the old packing shed. Soon I found my feet moving faster and faster until I was at full stride, running for my very life. I thought all sorts of beasts and monsters were trying to get me. Mine was really the Wolf waiting to trick me into a bad decision!

This I believe was the time, 1948, that our family fragmented and it was everyone for himself. Learn how to survive, or else! My Dad, who was always looking for jobs for me to work and make money, found me a job with the town baker who's shop was on Jeff Davis Ave. called the "Sweet Shop". For the next three and a half years I would learn a lot about dough and fishing and a measure of self-respect.

Mr. Paul Davis, the baker of Sweet and Not so Sweet things made from dough, was the best fisherman I ever knew. He caught more fish than he knew what to do with. Of course, all this was fueled with Stillbrook Whiskey, his favorite drink. I was 14 years of age and wet behind the ears!

All this because I worked for Doodle E. Squat.

It was better than being at home.

Wet behind the ears.

"Shoe Shine Mister?"

When I said my Dad and I didn't talk very much about things, I wasn't entirely truthful. In fact, we talked, or should I say he talked and I listened quite a bit about work. His philosophy was if you can get up out of bed, you could go to work - make money! Eureka! My Dad was a workaholic. He also had some other vices too!

He made me one of those shoe shine kits, the ones made of wood like you see in the old movies, ones that come on TV late at night, with a strap to carry it on your shoulder. It was a rectangle shaped box with a shoe rest on top for potential customers to place their scuffed and dirty shoes to be made like new again by my polish and cloths - my magic! The box part held the cloths and polishes, supplied by my father. It was my start in life so to speak, my inheritance. The rest was up to me. He said so!

I was eight years old. The year was 1943; the Second World War would be in full engagement. Hitler was giving Europe, Britain hell so to speak. I didn't know it yet, but Hitler was also gassing millions of Jews in special made ovens. A lot of them were children, some the same age I was. He lured them into baths, but clean water was not what came out of those pipes! Those children wouldn't get a chance to shine shoes, or go into business, as I was! - Or do anything at all. He closed all their peepholes! "Hi Ho, Hi Ho, It's off to work we go."

My youngest sister's peephole opened February 24, 1943. She would be the last child my Mother would reproduce. Her reproductive system was giving up. It would let her know it, too. Very soon!

I walked with my portable business slung on my shoulder, ten or twelve blocks to the main part of town, to seek dirty shoes. At that time Gulfport, MS, the business part anyway, was collectively in a Courthouse Square arrangement. Some kind of city planning!

There was the Great Southern Hotel close to the highway and the Gulf of Mexico, the park in front of that, the outdoor fruit and vegetable stand across the street. There were 13th and 14th Streets, North and South, and 29th to 24th Avenues, East and West - my business empire! Most of these old parks and buildings, not to mention the people are defunct now. Most of all the old-timers people's peepholes have closed! Did I mention that Gulfport had three movie theaters - How about that!

Blacks could only go to one theater - the Gulf Theater, and they could only sit in the balcony. Some of them had portable businesses like mine. I didn't realize the shoeshine businesses were so much in demand. I considered my Dad brighter than I first thought! They could make the shine rag pop in time to music they would sing or whistle! Boy! I sure was impressed. I secretly wished I was black - yas suh! I tried to make mine pop, but all I ever did was jerk out of my hands!

I made 37 cents my first day, 10 cents for each two shoe shines, 17 cents for doing a errand for some merchant delivering a package! I didn't know so much money could be made so easy. No one had to roust me out of bed the next morning. "The early bird gets the worm"! And the money too and the shoes to shine! And so on.

TRUE LOVE

I attended Gulfport Jr. High School. This came about because when in school at St. John's, my sister was insulted by someone in her class. He told her an F-- word, and when my mother got wind of this, she and the principal at St. John's had words. Then my mother slapped the face of the boy. All "Hell," so to speak, broke out. The next day when at school I was bullied by several boys of my own age and others. I got beat up - but not before getting my licks in on the instigators of this. (It would be many years before this was healed. Some of it would never be; some are defunct now.) But, it opened new doors for me to meet my first own very true love! A girl that to this day I still remember with special love and caring - My very first love. Her name was Barbara.

We met shortly after I enrolled at Gulfport Jr. High. I was 13 and so was she. We did not have Homeroom together. I wished many times then and now that we had. We would walk around the school on recess break or at lunchtime hoping to catch a glimpse of each other. - Ain't young love great? I wore this knit pullover cap on the back of my head. Boy, was I cool.

Her family lived on the West side of town on 32nd Ave. Her father was the manager of the only A&P Food Store on the Coast at that time in Downtown Gulfport. There was no Edgewater Mall, or the shopping centers there are now. Most all serious businesses were downtown - the four movie theaters. Now there are neither.

I do not remember if her mother worked outside the home or not at that time. She had a brother Charlie. He was two and a half years older than her. They had a farm near Saucier, MS. I was invited several times to go out to the farm with them where we rode horses and had picnics, or just walked and talked about things people 13 years old talk about.

She liked to walk holding hands window shopping. We did this quite a lot. She would rather do this than go see a movie or spend money. Westside Community Park was not far from her house; so many times we just went there. I know we kissed, I just wish I could remember.

My friend's father learned that he had a tumor growing on his brain causing him great pain and distorting his thinking. So one night after the A&P had closed and all employees had gone home to their families, he sat in his office and with a device made to propel steel projectiles, he sent them on their way by a mixture of sulfur, charcoal, and saltpeter fixed with a cap. He did what no doctor was able to do - remove the tumor, along with most of his head. Talk about medical progress.

I forgot to mention that after my maternal grandmother passed away, my Mom and Dad had itchy feet so to speak. So we began a long and tiring journey of moving and searching for something. God knows what? Maybe what causes their feet to itch! My family has Gypsy-in-my-soul feet. So, soon they needed to move again. We left for Long Beach. After moving to Long Beach, I sort of lost track of my friend. I do not know why to this day - for she has been in my head and my heart all these years.

Barbara Billingsley, would you care to go for a walk! - Window-shop a little maybe?

I miss you a lot!

I miss you a lot!

MY JOB AT THE BAKERY

This is what the sign outside of the pastry shop on Jeff Davis Ave. said:

Paul was the baker, the maker of things out of dough, and the drinker of Stillbrook Whiskey, and the fisherman of the Gulf Coast – The Old Man of the Sea. He had a boat; it was called "By George." His peephole has been closed a long time. I wonder what he's fishing for now?

He had a wife. Her name was Kathleen, but he called her "Amaryllis" after the flower. She was a large, brown-skinned woman of heavy design and questionable mental design. She

43

had a nickname by which she called me. Want to know what it was? She called me "Idigit". I think this to be because I worked so hard for doodle-squat, $13.50 a week – 7 days a week! She thought it to be funny. I did not! Still don't!!! Her peephole is closed, too! She lived a long time after Paul's peephole closed. Imagine that, and so on.

They had two children, a boy by the name of Randy and a girl by the name of Pottey. That was her nickname. Her given name was Patsy. Someone closed Pottey's peephole when she was living on the East Coast. Never did find out who. As far as I know, Randy's peephole is still open. I wonder if he can make things out of dough? I wonder if he likes Stillbrook Whiskey?

Paul's other favorit.
Pastime, , Stillbrook
Was the other, Well
Making things out of
dough, ranks up there
too!

FISHING, OR
PAUL, THE OLD MAN OF THE SEA,
AND ME

I think I always liked to fish – even before I met Paul Davis, and went to work for the Pastry Shoppe. The only difference was I didn't know the fine art and secret of being a good fisherman.

I had many pipe dreams, and some of them were made out of bread dough. These dreams made me to rise to most occasions. I was eager to learn the secret of how to make things out of dough. Like yeast is to flour and water, and salt and sugar in proper amounts. The proof is in the Proffer Box, so to say!

Paul was short, 5'6" with white hair, big round belly, red nose and cheeks. I always thought that if he grew a beard and put on a red Santa suit, he was a dead ringer for ole St. Snick. Ho, Ho, Ho, and Stillbrook away! He also looked a lot like the Pillsbury Doughboy – like Gaby did.

Paul had a big boat, the "By George." It got that named because a man named George built it. It was 28 1/2 feet long, 8 1/2 feet wide, and very deep. Made of marine plywood and good sturdy materials, its power came from Chrysler Wakine engine – 300 horsepower. It could run 42 mph on a good flat-water surface! The engine was an inboard-outboard, a new concept for the early 50's. We had a Spade 12 hp outboard, just in case the Chrysler gave out. To my knowledge, it never so much as backfired. Some power plant!

We made many trips to the outer island, stayed overnight often, ate Vienna sausages (straight out of the tin, and cold too) and crackers with Barq's drinks. Cold food we wouldn't look at twice back at home, but on the beach... Call me Ishmael!

Listen, we caught more fish than Carter has liver pills, so to speak; Speckled Trout, Red Fish, Flounder, Gray Mullet, White Trout, Skip Jacks, Spanish Mackerel, King Mackerel, Grouper, and fish with bright colors that I had never seen before or since, shark, too. Mostly sand sharks. But I've been close enough to touch some ten to twelve foot Hammerheads and White Tips, and so on. Once a shark came by Paul and took his whole string of fish, bait and all! Imagine that!

Paul had secrets stored away in his alcohol-hazed brain cells about how to catch fish, and I wanted to be the one to learn them – before Stillbrook shut down his power plant. I can say with all honesty and credit to Paul, that I never saw him drunk or unable to bake or fish or anything. Honest Indian! It did, however, later in his life, help to cause a diabetic condition and to lose his sight –

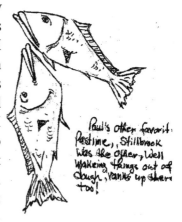

Paul's other favorit. Pastime,, Stillbrook was the other, Well making things out of dough, ranks up there too!

and later still his live, but not before he lost his right leg. Paul sort of became a loser of things, so to speak – He lost his memory, too. One time I was out of work, married with three children, needing money for Christmas. He said he couldn't pay much, but if I helped with all the holiday baking he would pay me minimum hourly wage for helping out. I agreed and worked steadily for the next four days. Maybe Stillbrook finally shut things down. Just my luck. I never was paid! Maybe it was time for me to pay for all those fishing trips.

Listen, we still had Christmas, and presents, and all that jazz. And I never brought it up to him, to Paul I mean, and he didn't either. God bless Stillbrook!

Have you ever caught White Trout using a piece of white handkerchief as bait? I did, big ones, too. Ain't that something-The old man and the sea and me.

"Something Fishey"

"Why Did You Go Away Grandmother?"

I really believe that had my Grandmother lived, the outcome of the whole family would have been different. Mary Anne began to show signs of mental illness as far back as 1945 and 1946. It was said that after the death of my grandmother, that the home on 19th Ave. made Mary Anne sick and impossible to live in. I don't know this to be true. I believe that mother and father used that excuse to sell a home that was paid for and move to Mississippi City to open his first dry cleaning shop. We moved to Mississippi City and stayed there for the next two - two and a half years. I had my first experience at St. James Catholic Church during this time. I was sorry to leave St. John's and my friends.

Note: From *July of 1946 until mid 1985, when I purchased a head stone, I remembered my Grandmother did not have one. I often wondered why my parents, in all that time - 36 or 37 years-never put a head stone on her grave. They could buy something to drink, but not a head marker - go figure!*

We live there on 19th Ave. from 1940 to 1946, during the Second World War. Shannon was born there and contracted viral pneumonia. She would have died had it not been for mother getting friendly with a Dr. by the name of Gerecei to get a new drug called penicillin, which saved her life. Remarkable what a mother will do for their child. Even hump the brains out of a medical man to save her child. Bet you did not know this, did you? If the government would have found this out, she could have gone to jail and the doctor would have lost his license to practice medicine! Their peepholes are both closed now, even my younger sister. I would have done this too!

I have to write in between household duties, shopping, cooking, playing music, making things out of clay and teaching some music, etc. "Speedy Delivery" you know. I often wondered if Tim and Edith really ever did enjoy each other. Well you could say they stayed together for a little over 50 years. Was it for *love* or *spite*? They could fight, curse, and make our lives a hell on earth, but I never remember my Grandmother raising her voice. Listen, I spent many a night on the cot at the front of her bed. I never felt so safe and loved in my life, even to this day. Summer days in the park, snow cones, ice cream, and just hanging out! Carousels, monkey bars, and swings-such was the gift of being a child. Too bad it could not last. "Come back my inner child!"

This was in the time of no TV or mass communication, only radio. We sat around evenings after supper and watched radio. *Let's pretend, The Green Hornet, F.B.I. in Peace and War, Jack Benny, The Inner Sanctum, Amos and Andy, The Fred Allen Show* and *George Burns* and *Gracie Allen*, just to name a few. Saturday evening my father would have a few beers and listen to the Grand Ole Opera from Nashville, Tennessee blue grass music. We even went to see little Jimmy Dickens one summer where out by the MS. Power Co. building is now in a big revival tent. My father was in hog heaven to say the least - fiddles and guitars and mandolins and piano in real life, I want you to know.

How I Became an Artist

Besides having pie in the sky dreams about making things out of dough, I also, as far back as I can remember, liked to sketch, draw, doodle, paint and work in clay, too. My best friend in 1949 was a boy named Gabe Brady. Gabe was a little overweight, while I was tall and slim. We were sort of a modern Laurel & Hardy, but we got along well. We would spend study hall time drawing cartoons and silly fantasy situations for our made up characters. After we had finished, we would get the other to critique, study, and grade our efforts. Gabe was also into amateur magic! Boy was I impressed. He taught me some magic!

He taught me how to make milk disappear in a newspaper funnel. I gave a magic show and made my family watch – and pay money to see me perform. Thanks Dad!

Our friendship was lessened when after 8th grade. Gabe went to St. Stanislaus in Bay St. Louis. It was where all good catholic boys were to complete High School – and to become something. Although I was doodling long before I met Gabe, our brief friendship impressed more pipe dreams for me. I daydreamed of becoming a cartoonist! Talk about ambition! It would be many years later before I approached painting again, but with a more sophisticated style and attitude. Bohemianism to say the least!

Gabe looked a lot like the Pillsbury Dough Boy.

What Gabe looked like to me.

PLAY IT AGAIN, SAM!

Somewhere around my mid-fifties, I did what up to that time I had only dreamed about. I bought myself an inexpensive guitar - Ephiphone - 133, division of the Gibson Guitar Co., made for people who could not afford doodle-squat. Well, let's go back 60 or 65 years. My Dad, being a product of country living and raising, played stringed instruments, as did most of his family - brothers, sisters, uncles, 1st, 2nd, 3rd, and so on cousins. I think you get the picture.

My Dad, who worked for Gulfport Laundry and Cleaning at this time, spent his Saturday nights like this; he would bathe and shave, put on his uniform for the next day, go purchase some beer, then sit by the radio. There was no TV in the early 1940's. He would tune everything to the Nashville Radio Network, and listen to The Grand Ole Opry broadcast from the Ryman Theater in Nashville, Tennessee, until late at night or reception gave out, or the beer gave out, and so on.

Every now and then between songs and performers, he would regale us with stories of how he and some of his brothers and cousins and friends would play all around the local counties for dances and such. Dad with his mandolin and guitar, oh, the trips they had! The things they saw and did! The girls! Life was so sweet. Play guitar, play!

I asked him many times to show me how to play the guitar, to show me some chords, but he was always too busy or had something to do. Later in life he would teach one of my sister's sons, maybe both of them to play. I resented him for this. So after much thinking, fretting and debating, I got a guitar of my own and a chord book and set out to teach myself.

And I did, too! I play very well now! Good enough to teach others to play their dreams.

SAFE SEX

It was very easy to be and remain a virgin in the 50's. Sex was mostly thought about and talked about, but only with a very close friend. Black and white TV with an antenna on the roof was just coming out and very few people had TV sets, no such thing as color TV. Mostly our entertainment was the movie show, *The Lobe Theater* on the Main Street, Jeff Davis Ave, or house parties. Those were big! Gulfport, the next town east of Long Beach, had three movie theaters. Imagine that! Had to catch a bus to Gulfport, then make sure you made the last one coming back after the movie or walk home – about three miles.

I don't think I ever so much as "felt up" a girl at any time, well, maybe one now that I think back, but this was when I was much older, say 17 or so. I was a virgin until I went into military service. Lost it down in Tijuana, Mexico, to some prostitute. It had to be the worst experience of my life at that time. I had fantasized moonlight, stars in the sky, our favorite song playing, locked in passion, love and desire – lust! I lost it to the tone of "Ain't you done yet," but with a Spanish accent. Imagine that! Boy did I feel empty!

Music held no charm for me at this time. Better things were yet to come!

Fred Welch

Ain't Life kind of great!
Hidey, Hidey, Ho!

THE GIRL OF MY DREAMS

It was also around this time that I met my future wife, the mother of my children. She did not attend the same school I did, Long Beach Public School. It was one long "L" shaped building that held all grades from first to twelfth. In fact, this was the only school in Long Beach, except for St. Thomas Elementary, a Catholic grade school. First through eighth grades were taught by the Sisters of Mercy, the parish I still live in and attend as to this day. Talk about progress! Talk about pipe dreams!

Lucy Nell Harrington – those were to become musical words to my ears – but not for a while. They would also return to my ears like thunder and hooves and the hot breath of some wild beasts, but this is much later, time is merciful. Girls now days in the 90's mature much faster than they did in the 50's. But even back then Lucy's build caught my eye. Dark curly hair cut short, soft brown eyes – great legs. So she was a dead ringer for a young Elizabeth Taylor. Really! A lot of people said so – mostly her family! What I didn't see, failed to notice, that along with her good looks she also was given, genetically speaking, a strong strain of insanity bequeathed by her mother's side of the family – something my own children hold against me to this day for reproducing.

Although I was innocent as a lamb, so to speak, as for my knowledge of this fact – ignorance of the fact is no excuse to my children. Some of them are afraid to reproduce to this day – can't say I blame them. Ignorance won't catch them napping! No sirree!

Talk about spice.

Innocence napping

FATHER O'MALLEY'S REJECTION

Before I met "Liz" and her dysfunctional family and not long after we moved to Long Beach, I took myself to the rectory of St. Thomas Church. I wanted to speak with the pastor there about the possibility of training and studying for priesthood. I walked up to the door and rang the bell. As I waited I wondered what to say to the pastor. The door opened and I met for the first time a Fr. Martin, who was in residence, however retired. He asked me what he could do for me. I told him why I had come by. He told me that I would have to speak with Fr. George O'Malley, as he was pastor in residence. So I waited while Fr. Martin went to the church to get Fr. O'Malley. After a short time, Fr. O'Malley came and we sat down and talked. I told him of my desire to become a priest. He listened and said we should speak more of this, so I would go at least once or twice a week to speak with him. We would work around the ground of the church and talk. I remained hopeful but a bit discouraged that I was not making progress in my pursuit to study theology and the like. So after many months of walking and talking and the like, I became discouraged and stopped going to the rectory, but it never left my heart or mind or spirit. Even now at the ripe old age of 71, I still think of what I could have been and done with my life as a Catholic priest, the pain and sorrow I could have been spared. My life would have been very different.

> "Saddest tales of mouth or pen
> Is that somehow it could have been."
>
> The poet
> Neicheie

I would never want to offend my children by what I just wrote, but I was never meant to be married - especially to "Liz" or the caretaker of my parents' lack of responsibility. But here I am. Lucky ole me! I have to deal with a lot of anger and resentment. My wolf has a lot of coats to wear! As I think about the situation, this is why I believe I took to painting and pottery and sculpting and maybe even playing music. Anything to keep me from thinking too much about how much I was misused! "My wolf never sleeps."

Who Are You and Who Am I

I think I mentioned my ex-wife looked a lot like Liz Taylor when she was young. Everyone says so! Mostly her family! Now she looks a lot like Rob Taylor, a guy who packs groceries down at the Sav-A-Center. He's short, fat, with a mustache. Imagine that! Time sure changes what we see!

Liz and I married, May 26, 1956 at St. Thomas Catholic Church in Long Beach, Mississippi, after a whirlwind courtship. I was working for General Electric, in New Orleans, whose motto back then was: *Better Living through Progress*. It was on all my uniforms, so it told me that everyday I went to work. We were company men, so I came to believe that statement – still do! I even wanted to deny that it wasn't so even during Vietnam – when G.E. made things that made life, not to mention progress impossible for people of yellow skin – talk about your faith being shattered! *Better things for better living through chemistry*. I didn't have a clue as to all this in 1956 through 1962 when I worked for them. I was busy working making money and babies with Lucy, my Liz. Happy as a clam, I thought!

Ronald Reagan worked for G.E. too. He hosted *The Westerner* on GE Theater, sponsored by General Electric. Lucy and I were building our nest. Lucy was building something else, too. She was encouraging her bad wiring and bad chemicals to deceive her and me, too. These bad chemicals and wiring would feed her to think I was plotting against her. She became an expert in bad wiring and thinking. She could have had a good job working for G.E. in their major appliance department – looking for bad wiring and so on. Other people believed her chemical induced thought pattern, too. Mostly her family who also thought she looked a lot like Liz Taylor. My, my!

Nine months later after our wedding and honeymoon at the Travel Lodge Inn on Airline Highway, New Orleans - owned by the way by Carlos Marsalis the local crime figure, now defunct (gets thicker and thicker doesn't it) – our fist child was born. We named him after me. He's nearly 50 now, making the Army his home. He likes to be called Joe. He signs his letter like this:

Art and talent run in the family!
And bad wiring, too – thanks to their mother and her
family, and mine, too.

Today I Became My Father

Today when I woke up, I made a sound that sounded just like my father, Timothy Henry Welch. Surprised me so, I had to look all around. My father's peephole closed on January 6, 1982. Bingo!

Mother's closed because of faulty plumbing in her vascular system. She would have much rather stayed. Dad, on the other hand, chose to have his closed. He accomplished this feat by denying his body food and sustenance along with, some powerful medications he was breathing for a chronic lung condition brought about by using for many years tobacco products, namely four packs of Camel cigarettes a day for forty years. So it really only took a small amount of effort along with some poor medical care from one of our local hospitals and doctors! Seem as though he had a wonderful plan all worked out, and I thought he was just an only country boy - some Yokel, huh! Quite the planner you were, Dad.

They are resting in St. Mary Cemetery, over in Bay St. Louis, Mississippi, the town where my mother was born. Her peephole opened November 14, 1910. Dad's opened January 10, 1914. Mine opened in Bay St.Louis on August 14, 1936. Lucy Nell Harrison Welch's peephole opened December 14, 1936. Father James Garcia Ward, C.M. is my pastor and friend.

His peephole opened May 17, 1950. My oldest sister's opened August 3, 1934 in Bay St. Louis, Mississippi, too. Imagine that! Hers closed July 8, 1985 at 7: 30 on a Monday morning. She was strapped to a hospital bed in a mental institution, Mississippi State Hospital at Whitfield, not far from Jackson, MS. I bet she didn't want to close her peephole, too! I think of this poem by Emily Dickinson, *A Country Burial*, when I think of her.

A Country Burial

Ample make this bed,
Make this bed with awe:
In it wait till judgment break
Excellent and Fair,
Be it mattress straight,
Be its pillow round:
Let no sunrise yellow noise
Interrupt the ground.

Emily Dickenson

Our family's plot looks like this:

How I Came to Work for the General Electric Company
Or
Progress Is Our Most Important Product

Around 1956 my Dad was tired of trying to sell Bond Bread, a company he was working for, and his route, that was out in the sticks, so to speak, Kiln, MS to be exact the very place he bought his supply of boot leg whiskey. He began to believe that New Orleans would be the better place to find happiness and money and all the good things of life. I think the alcohol had dimmed his switch so to speak, sort of like Paul Davis!

However, much to his credit, he did many years later, quit drinking and smoking, both at the same time. He would be hell to be around for about two months or so. I was very surprised that he and mother did not kill each other during this time! So God does not sleep!

He asked me to go with him to New Orleans. So me, being the dutiful son and also, secretly wanting to leave Long Beach agreed to go with him. We found a sparse, nosleazy apartment on the 2nd floor of an apartment building overlooking Canal St. We set up living in the "Big Easy"!

Dad and I were looking for work. Soon money, food, and excitement of the big city life began to wear off. I was discouraged but still hopeful. I went to the local employment office most everyday but nothing for me. Not even a bakery shop and me with all that experience of making things out of dough and all. Go figure!

One day as I was going to the employment office to check in. I was out of money and out of food. Being the good Catholic boy I was, I passed on Barrone St., the church of St. Joseph, and went in to say a prayer and visit. As I went in I noticed a poor box. Now let me explain that all Catholic churches had poor boxes to let people who were more well-to-do than me put money in! This particular box I gazed upon held a wad of folding bills that whoever put it in there did not push it all the way down into the box! The church was very quiet and no one but me and the rumbling of my empty stomach could be heard. There I was tempted to take the money, you bet I was. No more hunger, no more walking everywhere I went. It would solve all my problems at the time. All but one, my conscience! I reached up and taken hold of the money. I pushed it all the way down into the poor box. I said a short prayer and left the church, still hungry yes, but cleaner of soul, so to speak, for the time being! The brine of life is too much at times for me!

My Big Temptation

It was my day to check in with the caseworker at the employment service office and as I went in I signed the registrar and waited. When she caught sight of me she had a big smile on her face, she motioned for me to come over to her desk. As I sat down, she explained to me that she had a job for me to go and interview. She said it was only a part time job, but who knows, it could work into something. I said o.k. She gave me five dollars to have bus fare and something to eat. The world began to look rosy again.

As I left I felt full of hope. It would be many years before I would think of St. Joseph's Church and the poor box again. But, who knows? What do you think about that wolf? My wolf had horns! *That wad of money in the poor box was a test of my character and morals. God never sleeps!*

ME AND G.E.

I left the employment office, and the first place I passed served meals or breakfast. I went into the K&B drug store on the corner of Barrone St. and Canal St. Most all of them, the drug stores and the like, had a soda fountain counter that served breakfast and lunch. I sat down and ordered. Food never tasted so good! Not to mention the coffee.

Now with life flowing back into my body, I set off to find my interview and G.E. from Magazine St. to City Park to Bienville St to the 4300 block where the job of my life for the next six or seven years would be. At the time I did not know that.

My paper from the employment agency said I was to see a Mr. Serrea, manager of the major appliance Department. I went to the front desk and gave my paper it to the receptionist. She said to sit down and wait to be called.

I have to say my first impression of G.E. was a very positive one. I liked the look and the smell of the place. I heard someone call my name from the office and I got up and went in to see my potential boss for the next four or five years. Mr. Serrea and I hit it off from the very beginning. I liked him and he liked me. He explained that the job was only a part time in the parts department taking inventory with Mr. Chuck Sykes who was in charge of the department. So I went with Mr. Serrera through the parts counter, where customers came to purchase whatever parts they needed through the shop area, through the double doors to the parts department to meet Mr. Chuck Sykes. I liked Chuck from the very start. He had a good sense of humor and liked to smoke cigars. Hey! I was an Eager Beaver again! Chuck asked me all about myself as we worked to put this there and that there and supersede this and that and so on. I confessed that I only had so much money for bus and food. Chuck arranged for me to get an advance on my first paycheck. At this time I had no uniform yet. I wore my own clothes. I couldn't wait to get back to the apartment to tell my father about my day and good luck. He too had had a good day. He had been hired to work for another bread company, *Tip-Top Baking Company.* Not the best seller but a job. Now he could move my mother, brother, and sister to New Orleans and be together. Oh Happy Day!

As I left Bienville St. and G.E., I stopped and looked up at the signs on the building. This is what it said:

Progress Is Our Most Important Product

And I believed that too! Still do!

How pleased and relieved I was to wake up and have a definite purpose in life! I was a useful and a responsible taxpayer – one of many – giving hard earned money to the federal government to freely use or misuse.

My next year and a half of working in the parts department was a complete joy and learning experience for me. Chuck and me got along great. He learned he could count on me to do it right. I learned about parts, electricity and everything G.E. made at the time. I also learned about the shop next door and the people who worked there. The manager of the shop was an older man named Al Legnon. I got along great and learned a lot from him. At the time, I had no desire to leave the parts department. Chuck and I shared a liking for Jazz music and seafood on Fridays, especially around payday. He gave me a ride most of the way home!

I also had at that time a 1950 Buick that burned two quarts of oil to each gallon of gas. When I started the Buick, it fired and belched gray black smoke as it began to run. I sort of looked like the county mosquito man spraying for the stinging pests. No more buses for me! I got a lot of laughs and shots each evening when work was over, but I was still riding and not walking!

As I mentioned before after about two years, I was asked if I wanted a job in the shop department. I hated to leave Chuck and I talked to him of it. He said it would be

This symbol told me I was a company man!

a good chance for me and also more money. Anyway, I would always be coming back to the parts department for parts and special orders. So I agreed and took the change in jobs, and more money! I forgot to mention that now and for the past few years I have GE. Uniforms, Hidey Ho!

Because of Mr. Al Legnon, I learned how to fix broken major appliances and not be a parts changer. I've also have been given the opportunity to work on the transmission bench fixing drive units of washing machines and all the washers G.E. makes. When not fixing them or making new ones from scratch, I would work on anything that came into the shop – A/C units, refrigerators, freezers, dishwashers and so on. I was a wiz at fixing everything!

Later, when Liz and I were married and living on Piedmont Dr. in Gentelly, I would make all of our major appliances from scrap parts G.E. would throw away. I was happy as a clam at this time. God is merciful that I could not see into the future.

This is what a washer transmission looked like in 1956; most top-loaders had them.

After another two years or so, I was asked to work on the "unit truck"-A special truck that whose sole job was to go all over town and replace bad compressors from A/C units, freezers and refrigerators and anything else that needed fixing. I shared this job with a red-headed guy named Eddie Snakenberg. He was 6'4" and lanky at that time. He always gave up drinking beer for lent.

I have to say New Orleans was a great place to live and work in the 1950s and early 1960s. I used to have to drive through the city park to get to Bienville St. and G.E. I remember the New Orleans open Golf Tournament was first played there. I've seen all the old time great professional golfers that played there.

Another two years go by and I'm given my own truck to do service calls with. I'm married now and have two children, Fred (Joe) Welch Jr. and Lynn Marie Welch and of course "Liz" most of the time!

MUST HAVE BEEN SOMETHING I ATE

I was 23 and working for G.E. when my son Fred was a year and a half, and Lynn Marie Welch Steube was only nine months old. Lucy's bad wiring and bad chemicals had not thoroughly convinced her at this time that I was secretly plotting against her. At this time my own immune system was waging war with a bacterial agent I innocently picked up while shaving one morning. One has to be on guard at all times!

Lynn Marie Welch Steube is my oldest daughter. Her peephole opened on November 14, 1958. When I first saw her I thought she looked a lot like D. Eisenhower, our 34th president! He is now defunct! His peephole closed. Lynn is married now. Has been for over 24 years and has three children even though she expressed concern about the genetic probability she went ahead and began reproducing! Her husband Gary thinks all world, social and spiritual problems, and conformity of mankind, was probably my fault! What power I hold! My, my, I don't know my own strength.

I had somehow picked up a bacterial infection of the staphaccocia family, a strain of a bacterial infection. It was probably the cause of as many deaths on the battlefield in WWII as the carbon steel projectiles pierced vital organs fired by gas propelled firing implements, shot by men on all sides at each other thereby causing death. All sides fired them: Russia, Germany, Japan, all nations involved. Imagine that! Also at that time there were not many agents to combat or fight these relentless bacteria.

The war also caused some good, it made scientists find an antibiotic, Penicillin to fight staph, heal men, so they could get well and go back to killing each other. "Ring Around The Rosary!" My idea of how to fight a war - "Ring around the Rosary, the last man standing wins the war."

My Mother's peephole closed on November 11, 1982, which is also Armistice Day, (November 11, 1918), end of war to end all wars. Imagine that! Ended her own war! It is also Kurt Vonnegut's birthday, which is November 11, 1922. It has nothing to do with what I'm writing. I just thought you might want to know this bit of useful information.

I spent almost three months and ten days in a small hospital, St. Claude General Hospital in New Orleans. One of my doctors was a man from South America. His name was Dr. Poe. There would be many more. I'm written up, so to speak in the medical journal. My, my! Now *I'm* trying to write books.

The staph army that had invaded me was intent on full victory! Almost succeeded! I left the hospital almost three months later, more or less under my own power on November 11, 1959. Lynn would mark her first birthday three days later.

"Happy Birthday to You", Daddy's Home!"

How Staph Invaded Me and Made Me Ill, Life Holds a Big Surprise For Me!
Or
Never Use Other People's Medications!

The pimple I cut shaving.

One morning as I was shaving and getting ready for work, I noticed a big pimple on my chin. I didn't think too much about it so I shaved and left for work. I could keep my service truck at the house, a duplex I rented from Jack Gervious, who also worked for G.E. We had at that time radio-equipped communication to the office at base. I called in and got my work sheets for the day. I was to go over the bridge into Terrytown and fix some appliances. At that time, Terrytown was made up of G.E. inspired housing with mostly G.E. equipment. Well that day I kept reaching up and touching the pimple on my chin. It began to burn and throb. When I got home that evening I washed the spot and put iodine on the spot. I also used a salve that my mother-in-law had given to me to put on that infection. It had been used by her youngest son David who used it on his boils! Go Figure! Next morning it was puffed up and red and hurting, but I went on to work. It kept swelling and so I went in to see a doctor at the small hospital on St. Claude Avenue, the St Claude General Hospital. I was sent in to see a Dr. Poe. He looked at it and prescribed an ointment to put on it. As I look back, he should have taken a culture to find out what type of infection I was dealing with, but he did not. This went on for about a week, and everyday my face was more swollen and hurting. I began to look like a Halloween mask, grotesque and not human. I felt so bad now that on Saturday morning I asked Lucy to take me in to see Dr. Poe. He looked at me and said it was time to lance the spot and drain it. So he did. Nothing came out. By the time I left and returned home, I was in a state of shakes and going into convulsions.

Back I went to the hospital. They admitted me and put me in a ward with other patients. I was now going into pneumonia and pleurisy, and it was difficult to speak or breathe a word. The nurse came in to take a history and later told my mother and dad they did not think I would live through the night. I was 23 going on 24 years of age. In fact I had just made 23 in August. During this time it was September 10, 1959.

That night or early in the morning I went into a coma. I was aroused only to have the Last Rites of the Catholic Church. I was in a coma for about two and a half weeks at which time I died. This is what happened when I did.

My Journey in the Tunnel

I was aware of being in this dark tunnel and feeling very uncomfortable. Then I was aware of some being close to me. It spoke to me, mind to mind, for it was dark. It asked me with no emotion was I ready to die. I was thinking of this when it asked if I was pleased with the quality of my life up to that point. All this time I'm aware of others coming by me and going by me. Then my whole life up to that time passed through my awareness, from my earliest memory up to then. I saw some things that I did not like of my life. Now, big sins are important for a soul, but the ones I was more impressed with were the sins of omission and not loving and giving of myself and helping others. That word love that's in the Bible so many times is not there just to fill up spots in the book. One could not deny or rebuke anything that you are shown if it's not kind or good. All one would feel is remorse and shame. Now at this time I'm beginning to feel more comfortable in the dark of the tunnel and I seem to see a point of light at the end and I want to go to it. Then I hear the being ask me again, "Are you ready to die?"

I then think of my two children, but not once my wife. I tell the being that I fear no one will love and protect my children like I would. I would never see them grow up, go to school, marry and have children. No one would love them as I would. I just cannot go. I remember some things and some I do not! This I do remember, I'm in some place and it's so very beautiful, there is light, however not light from the sun. There is water and waterfalls and as the water flows it makes a beautiful sound and there are flowers that have a fragrance not on earth. I remember people in white robes and their faces shine with a glow. I'm now speaking with one and I ask if there are other worlds and they smile and say "Of course". I ask how to get to them and they say all you have to do is think of it and you will be there.

I think of the things of earth and troubles and strife, and it's all so simple to make better. Its pettiness and troubles could be fixed so easy, I think. Why can't we figure this out when we are there?

I'm sure I was shown a lot more, but it was taken from my memory. When I was sent back, they told me I was not ready to be there. Then I am back in the hospital. I was in this state of coma for about 2 1/2 weeks. Sometime during that event, my mother said I sat up in bed and said I think I'm going to make it!

Looking back at my age now I can see I had much more to suffer and deal with. I've made the statement at times that I have been blessed with bad health! I think my wolf has horns too!

I spent three months and ten days in St. Claude General Hospital. I made many friends and heard some pass away. I went from 162 pounds to 80 pounds. I had over 285 single injections, not to mention the constant drips and IV's, which made all my veins collapse. A pediatrician was called in to start an IV in my foot, the only vein they could use at the time.

I had on my case, the head of the LSU Tulane Medical School that came to take notes – a Dr. Seebury. He wrote me up in the medical journal, also a Dr. Lake from Gulfport who taught at LSU one day of the week came by to see me. I remember he stood at the foot of my bed and said; "You know you are not going to make it." I told him I would out live him and I did too! Well, He did offer some helpful medical advice, thanks to my ex-mother-in-law who at the time was a practical nurse taking care of his mother. So she came to St. Claude General and in my small room they put in a cot and she stayed there to clean me when I broke out in perspiration and everything on me and my bed had to be changed. She would also force me to eat when I couldn't stand the smell of food and when I coughed up puss and blood. That would make anyone else gag! She passed away last December. She had her faults, like the fact that for many years Lucy and probably Clara and others where molested by their father. She turned her head and just pretended it did not exist. Talk about brine.

This explains the many trips Lucy made when we were first married, back to the coast, and do not expect an explanation. I did, but never got one, only silence and indifference!

After three months and ten days, I left the hospital. I had made the promise that I had walked in and would walk out. Well, I did with some help on each side of me to hold me up. I also had to learn how to walk and move my limbs again!

It took over a year to get most of my strength back and return to work at G.E. Better things are ahead for me! I'll tell you more about this later.

What I've told you about the after death experience – Is there life after life? I've read a few books on this subject and some PBS specials. It helped me to deal with what I wrote about. I would not talk or mention to anyone of this for over 25 years. A friend convinced me to put it in this book. Thanks to you my friend!

When I did return to work at G.E. we had a new manager, Julian Johnson from Texas. Actually he looked a lot like President Johnson. He made life for me difficult at best to work at my job, sending me to the most difficult and hardest and dirtiest jobs he could find. The man was a heartless bastard and prick. If he's dead I wonder if it's hot where he is?

Some time ago I wrote a book called *A Call to Holiness*, published by *!Universe publishing*. I did not put this story in the book or the one about how I came to know the name of my Guardian Angel "Uriel". I will also write more about this later in this book.

I've always been sad about being forced to leave General Electric whose motto was and is "Progress Is Our Most

Fred Welch

Important Product". I had found my home, so to speak, with G.E., my friends and all the benefits, insurance, stock, a member of the Cajun club and many other benefits. But that bastard, Julian Johnson, the devil himself made it his vocation in life to force me to leave. He told me so! Well, I hope you're at peace, you prick!

Mid-life Crisis

I think most of the time many of us, completely miss the point. E.B. White's story about Wilbur the pig, entitled *Charlotte's Web* points this out. Wilbur is not the wonderful bright, star he's made out to be. It is the spider, Charlotte, who is wonderful and so on. She's the one spelling out how great the pig is and so on! Unselfish to the end!

Midlife is somewhat like this. We find our attitudes, values and morals challenged and are easy to become confused. We know that we are not young anymore, but deny that we are getting older - our fear of the unknown. Also there are other changes. Hair grows in the most unusual places and decides to stop growing on the top of our head, especially if you are male, sometimes female! If you are female, along the way you lose things, like your ability to house and produce children. Hair will grow in places you would rather not have hair. Razor blade commercials take on a brand new meaning for you!

I was not bothered or concerned with midlife until I reached the age of 55. Midlife can be the stereotypical man - shocking all, buying a red Porsche' and hanging around the local playground. It can also be a general feeling of dissatisfaction of not being content with each new day or one's self. Well, so I won't hit a homer today. Maybe I'll only just get on base! Or maybe I'll strike out, fall flat on my face. What happens after this is the real measure of man. Can I just accept it and laugh at myself, or do I rail and rant at life, God, the world and so on! Acceptance is easy to spell, but oh so hard to live!

I have a brother, Michael Henry Welch, five years younger than myself. He began to deal with midlife crisis at the tender age of 32 or so. His anger at his immediate family was and still is too painful and difficult to accept. I believe he will be a good priest. I pray for this, but mostly that God's will be done. He's back in the seminary at this time at St. John's of Camarillo, California!

Just for the record, I also had a younger sister, Shannon Marie Welch Hernandez, who before she married was a novice in the Convent of the Holy Family. They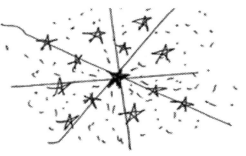

Twinkle, twinkle little star, how I wonder what you are!

had a Carmel in North Louisiana, Shreveport, to be exact. Shannon was there for about seven years and then for reasons I do not know, left and became a civilian once again. Her tragic life would make a book in its own. This younger sister passed away on November 30, 2005, three days after Katrina decided to level everything from New Orleans to outside Mobile, Alabama. There was especially a lot of destruction to the city of Long Beach, Mississippi, a place where I still live. I stayed with her in her hospital room, room 417, until her peephole closed. I wish I could have done more for my sister. She did have the Last Rites of the Catholic Church, thanks to my pastor, Fr. Louis Lohan. Shannon never did stand on convention so to speak. She could knit and crochet beautiful things.

I think she tasted the brine of life too much!

MARY ANN

I mentioned before my oldest sister and her journey through life, born August 3, 1934 in Bay St. Louis, MS, in an old home that now is a dance studio. She and I began our formal education at St. John's Elementary School in Gulfport, MS, she in 1939 and me the next year in 1940.

I really believe that my sister's bad wiring and odd thinking came with the 23 chromosomes from my mother's side of the family! My mother blew hot and cold, and you never knew what one you would find her in!

After we moved to Long Beach in 1949, some time around 1951 or so, she met Don Bell who was 4 or 5 years older than her. I would guess he was 21 at that time. He was in the air force stationed at Keesler Field in Biloxi, MS. I'm not sure how they met, maybe at some dance. Mary Anne loved to dance and anytime there was a dance, she would go. Of course, mother went along to chaperone and watch out for her. Anyway, Don Bell set his heart, body and mind on my sister. He wanted to marry her and nothing would do until he did. I have to say, I did at first take a liking to Donald Bell. He had some relations in Selma, Alabama, and I recall one time we made a trip there in a 1951 Buick convertible Don had at the time. My mother was always ready to go on an adventure. It didn't matter where or when. There goes that Gypsy soul again. No grass was going to grow under her feet. No sir! Not her!

Well Mary Anne and Donnie, as he liked to be called, hitched up and married. I bet if he could have seen into the future of my poor sister's bad wiring and chemicals, he would have still been driving that Buick convertible. Some of us get a break or luck, or whatever you want to call it, others are always at the airport when their ship comes in, so to speak. It was that way with my sister. Sorry to say, unfair. Yes, for I do not think, I knew a more loving, giving, and helpful person, when she was not held in the grip of bad thinking and manic behavior. She spent most of the rest of her life in and out of mental hospitals. Yet, she did reproduce, two sons, Jerry Bell and Michael Bell. The first one, Jerry, made sport and fun of his mother at every chance. Michael, on the other hand, lived with my mom and dad most all his life, as did Mary Anne. She gave into every whim and want that Michael had. He went to St. John's too, but then there were no more nuns to teach kids and no more rulers to hurt their hands. Too bad, Michael did not know what he missed.

Oh, what about Don and Mary Ann? Well, time is merciful and kind. So, after about ten years, they divorced. Here's what went down. Don left the air force and they settled down in New Orleans, then across the river in Marrano, LA. This is what Don did for Mary Anne. He knew someone in the drug business and got Mary Ann hooked on this and that. Ain't love grand?

Donnie bell worked for Sunbeam Bread Co., the best selling bread in and around New Orleans, both sides of the river. I think he stole more money from the bread co. than he made for them! He had connections with every store he went to on the route! I really believe he hoped Mary Ann would overdose and kill herself. If he could have seen into the future, all he had to do was wait. Mary Ann's many visits to this mental institution and that one would eventually land her into the state hospital at Whitfield, MS. The staff and doctors would do for him what he tried to do for so long. On July 8, 1985, strapped to a bed, she was forced to take medicines that caused her heart to stop and at the ripe old age of 52, like someone else to know, she stopped the war and left this vale of tears! Fly home little Bird!

Oh, how did she end up at that hospital? Well, it was thanks to her youngest son, Michael who signed her in and then left the state. To this day I do not know where he is!

So, there my poor sister sat for over two or three years. I wrote her as often as I could and sent some money and things every now and then. I even tried to have her placed in my care, but could not because of her son. All I could do was hurt and feel guilty. You know at this time I still do. The moral of this story is if you can do for someone in your family, please do it. No one is perfect and the guilt you will have to live with will not be worth it! Mary Ann died at the same age as my maternal grandmother at 52. That's salt and spice and a lot of Ginger.

And tears too!

Did I tell you she could bi-locate? *Bi-location means the ability to physically be in one spot or one place and spiritually in another.* I found this out at her wake from a priest who met her. My brother, who was in Houston at the time, saw her too the morning of July 8, 1985 at 7:30 a.m., that's when she went to heaven! I heard her screams of anguish and anger as she passed the home where I live now! She was too good for the world. One day I hope to see her again!

I hope she still loves me and forgives me for not doing more for her.

"American National Insurance Company and Me"

After being forced to leave General Electric Co. in 1962, I or I should say me and "Liz", and the two children moved back to the Gulf Coast. I really did not have any idea what I would do. I had made no inquiries or sent out any resumes. We stayed in a duplex house owned by my mother-in-law. I did qualify for unemployment, so we were not completely without funds. I have to say it did take quite a while for me to resolve my anger and resentment at Julian Johnson that prick. So after a while I began to look into work. I first thought about all the hands on experience I had gained with G.E., so I looked into places like Sears, McDaniel's Appliances and several other places that did the type of work I had been doing. Actually I'm still dealing with the heavy toll from what the staph infection had done to my body. It would be years before I knew just how much damage it had done to me and my general health – sugar and spice!

1. I worked for 6 months with Sears
2. I worked for about 2 weeks for McDaniel's
3. Now, along comes my father, the finder of Jobs, the workaholic.

He, mom and my sister Mary Ann and her two sons, Jerry and Michael were still in New Orleans. However, more itchy feet syndrome was to come for them. "Fred," He said over the phone, "I have a job for you with Tip-Top Bread Co.". Here's what I had to do: Get up at 1:30 a.m. in the morning and dress and drive to New Orleans by 4:30 a.m. to take my bread truck out. My first stop was at the parish prison in the heart of New Orleans, run by Sheriff Foley!

I have to catch you up at this point. When "Liz" and I first married I had the second best 1956 Ford Hardtop convertible in the city. A guy I worked with, Ronnie Smaltz had the first one. His was solid white and loaded, mine was peppermint green and white – dual, Hollywood glass, packed mufflers and many other fancy items like skirts and spinner hub caps and more. A long way from that 1950 Buick, you bet! I did however find a 1950 Chevrolet coupe that looked good and better still. Ran well and no smoke! Things are looking up so to speak. So my trips to New Orleans were without incident or breakdowns. See, my angel was looking out for me, and I never knew it at the time. Thanks Uriel!

I have to say I really did like working for Tip-Top Bakery Co. I just wish the bread sold much better. It never did! But I was there with Dad and for a short time with my brother-in-law, Don Bell until he went with Sunbeam the best seller in New Orleans. Tip-Top Bread Co. had an inner city baseball team. I had played on the one with G.E. for several years. I liked the game, still do. I root for the Mets but they blow hot and cold, mostly cold at this writing.

I made good money for that time, and I also played the horses at the fairground racetrack and made a few bucks every now and then. Lucky ole me, do-da-do-da day!

I would bring back to the coast cases of baby food and toys and gifts. The baby food went mostly to "Liz's' Sister Clara who got knocked up buy a 2nd Lt. In the air force. His name is Jeff Dobbin. I later got him a job with American

National Insurance Co. but after a while he forgot what money belonged to the company and what was his. More about this later.

I came home one Friday. Now, we were living in our own rental home and Lucy was even more withdrawn than usual. I asked her what was the matter. She would not answer.

When I was a younger man, I can tell you that I was not blessed with a lot of patience, so after going off like Mount St. Helen's she told me that her father Michael Harrington had tried to molest our daughter Lynn Marie (five years old at this time). I wanted to kill the bastard, but after a while I cooled down. She, "Liz", said she told her father to get out and never come back. The bible says, seven times seven to forgive. It would be many years before I put two and two together, that the reason for Lucy's bad wiring and chemicals was due to being molested by her father. Her mother knew of this and just turned her head to it all! What you do not see won't hurt you.

I found out later that he had tried this on Lucy's first cousins who had to stop coming by because of his crazy behavior. I believe he also molested Lucy's sister Clara, maybe the sons Cleve and David Harrington, who knows. Lucy's mother said it was because of his brain tumor he had. It was cut out at a hospital in New Orleans, the same place, where Gary cooper had his tumor removed – like sour milk, lemon juice, and chili peppers, flakes! Not spicy enough? There's more to come and people wonder why I have heart disease! Hidey, Hidey, Ho, Ho, Ho! This is when I decided to find a home around the coast area.

We had a small Industrial policy with AMIC, (American National Insurance company). A Mr. Irwin Weems was the manager and he was collecting the debit looking for good, honest, people to hire. Actually, it was the very same debit that one day (because of me) Jeff Dobbin would call his private spending ground – but that would be later.

By – the – bye we now have three kids now. So much for doctors theory that I would be sterile for the rest of my life because of the staph infection and all the meds and drugs I had to take. So much for that theory! I wonder at times if any of my children are really mine, mostly when I'm pissed at them. You see Lucy was banging everyone and anyone but me. Desperation drove me too her bed. It never occurred to me to have an affair. Between my conscience and my catholic faith it was not in my agenda.

I would give Lucy our car, a 1962 V.W. Bug, fill it up with gas and oil and give it to her one day a week to just go out and do whatever (not whoever) she wanted, with no explanation to me. She would come back late at night, the VW would be almost out of gas and oil and never a word of thanks or anything. I never asked and she never told. Talk about dumb dough!

So I took the aptitude test for the insurance co. and physical. I passed with flying colors, and Mr. Irwin Weems and I went on my two-week training period. How to dress for success, how to knock on the door and what to say, how are you today? Want to buy more life insurance and so on!

Most people paid for the month by check. Some put cash – industrial premiums and MDO monthly debit ordinary policies! Try to, in the course of the day to cold canvas, knocking on strange doors and making afternoon appointments and such!

I got pretty good at this. After a while I was the leading agent in five states! I won many awards. See, I'm an eager beaver again! My books were always in the best shape they could be. No losses and advances in all areas of collections.

For the first four or five years I really enjoyed the challenge of selling, but if I could have seen the "dough rising", so to speak, I would have looked for other ways to support my family. Stress of home and stress of trying to be the best at the insurance game finally got to me. I had a partial meltdown! But more drugs took care of that and pretty soon I was my usual eager beaver self again! Bake that barge and lift that pie! Life's got more for you to do, so get your ass out there and get with it little man!

It's not that I don't expect my many crosses in life or the weight of these. At times they seem to overwhelm me and drag me down. What gives me concern is that maybe one day or time I will just want to give up!

> *Roll that dough and bake that bread*
> *and get that shit right out of your head!*

I don't think the poet Nichicie said that! He did say and I quote "If we fail to learn by our mistakes, we are doomed to repeat them over and over again" end quote. You bet!

I believe the insurance job was an excuse to get away and stay away from crazy stuff at home, with "Liz" and her family you know! As I look back on the day out Lucy had with the V.W., she could have at least charged for her services, so to speak, it could have helped with family finances! God knows we could have used it. I had sex with Liz maybe 10 or 12 times in the 18 years we tolerated each other. This was no marriage. Even the Catholic Church didn't think so. It gave me an annulment years later.

I worked my tail off for the next 7 or 8 years for the insurance co. But I always knew that there was something fishy going on at home or somewhere on the coast. My mother never did trust Lucy and said so on several occasions! I do not remember any real closeness on their parts! There's a lot more I could write about and one day I will, maybe another book.

"Something Fishy"

93

Fred Welch

You see I'm a survivor, always was and always will be. I didn't know it at the time but the best part of my life was yet to come. Well, we'll exclude the health stuff – didn't do so well in that. The outstanding women that I would meet and learn about, love and sex and the things I did not have before- how to laugh at life and myself and listen, yes even love!

1. I returned to college – two times.
2. I've studied art and have painted for over 40 years – sold some and met many artists.
3. I tried pottery and ceramics.
4. I've done sculpture
5. I've written and published a book, maybe two!
6. I play music, Jazz and good music.
7. I teach others to play, and I teach art too!
8. I have many special friends.
9. I cook very well, thank you!
10. I'm grateful to God, for the well being of my children and their ability to care for them selves and their families.

Looking back down the road of life, I have been very fortunate and blessed to experience so much of this life, pain and all! Most of this as I stated in the beginning, I do not intend to think about again. My attic, so to speak, is mostly cleared out. There was a lot of junk in there.

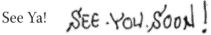

So now Gingerbread man what shall we write about now? And where is the wolf?

See Ya!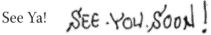

How I Came To Know the Name of My Guardian Angel

Have you ever wondered if you do indeed have a guardian angel? Many people do and so did I. For many years I would pray and ask Father God, "Do I really have an angel?" This prayer went along for over 10 or more years. But whenever I went through my prayer life, I would always ask, but no answer or reply.

When I was a small boy and my maternal Grandmother was with us, she gave to my oldest sister Mary Ann and me this picture of two children crossing a bridge with no hand rails to hold on too or stop you from falling off the bridge down into the rocks and water below. Behind them is this angel with her arms outstretched to catch them and help them across the bridge – their guardian angel. I still have this picture in a frame to this day. It's in my bedroom. I treasure this picture for many reasons! I think of my Grandmother often and with much love and gratitude.

Well, this one day as I was praying I asked Father God, again, I said; "If it's o.k. with you, do I really have a Guardian Angel?" I didn't really expect to get an answer, why should I? Then as clear as can be, I heard in my inner spirit, "My name is Uriel". I was shocked and surprised to say the least. I thought maybe it was just me and my own thoughts that said that. Then as I was thinking; "I wonder how you spell that name?" I heard just as before, "U.R.I.E.L", spelled out for me by this inner voice! I was speechless and overjoyed and many other feelings. I didn't tell anyone of this for many years, but I always said a special prayer to my guardian angel, Uriel! Still do. I listen for his voice and if I pay attention and avoid sin and distraction, he warns me of the spiritual harassments by the other side. I'm the better for it. The wolf never sleeps!

Still, I kept this to my self for many years. Then this one particular time I was over to some Jewish friends home for dinner and I felt the need to share with them about the angel story and how I came to know Uriel.

As I recounted the story I just shared with you, I was talking and sharing when one of the daughters excused herself from the table and left. We were talking and sharing when the daughter Khanna came back and in her hands were several pages of computer print outs about the Guardian Angel Uriel. She handed them to me and as I read I was in absolute sheer amazement by what I read.

The print outs, told me of the arch angel Uriel and his contributions in the bible. He was called by several names, sent by God to do this and that and many things. He was the angel that wrestled with Samuel all night long, for one explanation and there are many more, examples of his obedience to God the Father, and doing the work sent by "Him".

I do not think of myself as anything special or deserving of the blessing and how do I prove it? To me it's really all a matter of faith. As I wrote in my first book *A Call to Holiness*, if you believe, no explanation is necessary. If you do not, none will suffice. So there is the story. I continue to pray to my special angel, for his help, protection and to guide me.

If I listen to his voice, I stay out of trouble. If I do not, I end up in the deep muddy! So pray and who knows, you may learn your angel's name! Sweet as a cinnamon bun!

Today I saw Pete Bertin Again
Or
Remember the Great Chicken Caper of 1946

I needed to make a grocery stop at our local Winn-Dixie today. I parked on the side of the store and went in. I only needed a few things - bread, milk and some bananas and got them, paid and started out. As I approached my truck, I looked over next to me in the next lane and thought I recognized the man sitting in the passenger seat. He was smoking a cigarette and looking straight ahead; as I walked over he turned and looked at me, a smile started on his lips. He knew who I was. I went over and started to shake his hand.

Some time ago maybe in the late 1980's, Pete had been in a bad auto accident. While recovering from it he had a stroke that left him with limited use of his right side and the inability to speak clearly. He knows what someone is saying, but does not have speech as most of us do. It comes out as "dip, dip, dip,", all the time using his hand to point or gesture. I pretend to read him, so to speak, but I really do not understand him. I brought up the time we had the great chicken caper killing.

I could tell by the look on his face he did remember this awful act. This crime of ours, our dance with insanity! After a bit I told him that Great Grandmother Capdepon probably forgave us and everything was all right. He gave a nod and I told him to be good and that I was glad to see him again. He smiled and I went to my truck a bit sad and left.

This is what her chickens looked like before me and Pete rearranged their form and feathers and molecules, with the help of the pigs of course.

Somehow this brought back to me when I won my child custody suit for the welfare of my three children. Joe (Joey) was old enough to make another decision to live with someone else, not his mother or with me. However, I did get Lynn, Chris, and Wendy. We found an upstairs apartment on Girard Avenue. You could see the beach and Gulf of Mexico out our bedroom window. The best part was when I came home from work and we had our supper meal and it was time for bed. I cannot tell you the tender feeling I would have when I would look over at them asleep in their beds. I knew they were safe. What love I felt for them and gratitude to God for this blessing! For the next four to five years I had no personal life of my own and I do not regret it. I went to work and could not wait to get home or shop for supper and watch them grow and I would try not to betray their trust in me. If all fathers would do such as this, they would get to know their children in a much deeper and special way - what women have known for ages. "Good night my children, if only you knew how much your Father loves you!"

This is how I came to have my children. In 1972, Lucy's family had convinced her that I was her biggest problem and she should divorce me and get the children, the house, the car and whatever we had in the bank, also all the furniture too. Her sister found her an attorney to take me to the cleaners. Although he did at the time, he would later be indicted for fraud and stealing from trust funds and be disbarred – time, the great healer. So I paid my child support as ordered by the court. I looked forward to my visitation times. On this one particular time, a few months later, I showed up for my visit, check in hand and said I was ready to go out with my children. Lucy and her mother just looked at each other and did not say a word. I asked again - "Where are the kids?" No answer. Finally Bernice, Lucy's mother, said that they had to place them in foster care in a fundamentalist Baptist Children's home way out on Highway 49. I asked how come no one bothered to talk to me about this. As usual, no answer. I asked where this home was and how to get there and who was in charge. I got some answers, but not too much help. I left there with a sinking sick feeling in my stomach.

I went out to the home. I look back now and know that between my leaving Lucy's other home and my finally getting out there, her family had alerted the preacher I was coming. They had also filled his head with a lot of misconceptions and lies! So when I did get out to the home, he was in a state to tear me a new one. I knew it was of no use, so I left not knowing if my children were o.k. and not being abused.

I found me an attorney and started a long, painful, and expensive legal suit to get my children. You know all my ex-wife had to do was sign them over to me and they would have been out of there that day. But no. She was under the spell of her mother, sister and others. I'll spare you readers a lot of stuff that took place out at the children's home! It was not nice or good for them! It took a year and a court trial and a lot of money, but I did get custody of my children - not to mention the stress to me! And people wonder why I have heart trouble. My ginger is a lot spicier than you know! It's good for everyone that I am not a violent man.

Just for the record, all my children have done well considering. They have homes, good jobs, and take good care of their children. I do not see them often, but my boys call and visit on occasion. My youngest, Wendy, has not done well with relationships. She is on her second divorce. My oldest, Lynn, still bears a lot of guilt and resentment, mostly aimed at me. Well, she cannot blame "Liz" can she? A mother could be "Lizzie Borden", but to a child she can do no harm! It's not the same for fathers. Too Bad!

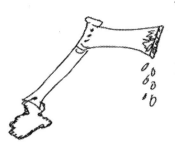

Lizzie Borden took an ax and
gave her father 40 whacks,
Then she gave her mother 41!

Epilogue

I've loved,
which was PURGATORY.
I've lost,
which was HELL
And I've Survived,
This I believe to be HEAVEN!

From *How to Survive the Loss of a Love*

Listen, when I began this book, almost 38 years ago, and life had kicked me about, so to speak, I was wearing a suit of anger and didn't want to take it off.

Years of therapy and at times wearing my close friends out, I thought, surely there must be other ways to face one's fiercest misgivings!

I have always been one to put pen to paper so to speak, so I kept a journal. I didn't write all the time, but when I did the words seem to flow from me. So every now and then I would write. My lack of writing was only because at the time and for many years I had been a painter of fine art, a potter, sculptor and teacher of the classical guitar.

I also played music with some of the choirs at my church, for house parties and art openings. I even put together my own jazz trio, *The Sonny Welch Trio*. So my time to write was put on the back burner for a good while. "I'll do that later", I would tell myself.

Now putting most of the above away, I now only want to write about what I see or think I see. The "wolf" has been in my head for too long! Clearing the junk out will give me the room and opportunity to get to the wolf! I may throw him out, I may make him dance, or I may make a pet out of him.

Let me explain the poem in front of this chapter:

I've loved:
I thought I married my soul mate, the one who would be by me throughout our life. Others would come by but not to stay for the long haul!

Don't count on your children or grandchildren being there, not even your friends or strangers. When you stop and look around, it will only be you!

I've lost:
All of you, like me, have had to deal with loss! Loss of hair, loss of a loved one, loss of a job, a loss is a loss. Those stages of loss as described in psychology we deal with!

I've survived:
This one is very special to me. I think I am the stronger and better for it by just keeping on doing, living, and dealing with life on the terms it gave me that day. After all, what else can you do? To give up is unthinkable. Anything short of getting up and moving on is not an option to me. I refuse to let the wolf win. Today a truck brought me some copies of my first book *A Call to Holiness.*

This is what the side of the truck said:

See how my art training has served me well! And I thought I would not use it again.

About the references to people, products and the like; I in no way intend to disparage, or make light of the fine products. I use many of them in my day to day living. They are good and useful and make our living the better for it; also the people, living or dead that I knew or tried to know in my journey on the road of life. I miss most of them a lot and hope they are in the hands of God!

And to you, the readers of my books, I thank you very much. I wish you peace, love and Health!

Fred Welch